THE
49-DAY
EFFECT

A DON'T-BREAK-THE-CHAIN INSPIRED
HABIT TRACKER

HOW TO USE THIS BOOK:

I. Write the daily habit you want to make or break at the top of the page.

2. Write your "why"s - your reasons for doing this, what is motivating you to do this habit each day.

3. For each day you're successful in achieving your habit, use a bright-colored marker to strike an X in the box.

4. Keep your habit chain going daily for 49 days. As an added challenge, try not to miss more than 1 day in a row.

5. We recommend sticking to 3 habits maximum.

6. Happy habit building!

THE HABIT:

YOUR "WHY"S:

THE HABIT:

YOUR "WHY"S:

THE HABIT:

YOUR "WHY"S:

THE HABIT:

YOUR "WHY"S:

THE HABIT:

YOUR "WHY"S:

THE HABIT:

YOUR "WHY"S:

THE HABIT:

YOUR "WHY"S:

THE HABIT:

YOUR "WHY"S:

THE HABIT:

YOUR "WHY"S:

THE HABIT:

YOUR "WHY"S:

THE HABIT:

YOUR "WHY"S:

THE HABIT:

YOUR "WHY"S:

THE HABIT:

YOUR "WHY"S:

THE HABIT:

YOUR "WHY"S:

THE HABIT:

YOUR "WHY"S:

THE HABIT:

YOUR "WHY"S:

THE HABIT:

YOUR "WHY"S:

THE HABIT:

YOUR "WHY"S:

THE HABIT:

YOUR "WHY"S:

THE HABIT:

YOUR "WHY"S:

THE HABIT:

YOUR "WHY"S:

THE HABIT:

YOUR "WHY"S:

THE HABIT:

YOUR "WHY"S:

THE HABIT:

YOUR "WHY"S:

THE HABIT:

YOUR "WHY"S:

THE HABIT:

YOUR "WHY"S:

THE HABIT:

YOUR "WHY"S:

THE HABIT:

YOUR "WHY"S:

THE HABIT:

YOUR "WHY"S:

THE HABIT:

YOUR "WHY"S:

THE HABIT:

YOUR "WHY"S:

THE HABIT:

YOUR "WHY"S:

THE HABIT:

YOUR "WHY"S:

THE HABIT:

YOUR "WHY"S:

THE HABIT:

YOUR "WHY"S:

THE HABIT:

YOUR "WHY"S:

THE HABIT:

YOUR "WHY"S:

THE HABIT:

YOUR "WHY"S:

THE HABIT:

YOUR "WHY"S:

THE HABIT:

YOUR "WHY"S:

THE HABIT:

YOUR "WHY"S:

THE HABIT:

YOUR "WHY"S:

THE HABIT:

YOUR "WHY"S:

THE HABIT:

YOUR "WHY"S:

THE HABIT:

YOUR "WHY"S:

THE HABIT:

YOUR "WHY"S:

THE HABIT:

YOUR "WHY"S:

THE HABIT:

YOUR "WHY"S:

THE HABIT:

YOUR "WHY"S:

THE HABIT:

YOUR "WHY"S:

THE HABIT:

YOUR "WHY"S:

THE HABIT:

YOUR "WHY"S:

THE HABIT:

YOUR "WHY"S:

THE HABIT:

YOUR "WHY"S:

THE HABIT:

YOUR "WHY"S:

THE HABIT:

YOUR "WHY"S:

THE HABIT:

YOUR "WHY"S:

THE HABIT:

YOUR "WHY"S:

THE HABIT:

YOUR "WHY"S:

THE HABIT:

YOUR "WHY"S:

THE HABIT:

YOUR "WHY"S:

THE HABIT:

YOUR "WHY"S:

THE HABIT:

YOUR "WHY"S:

THE HABIT:

YOUR "WHY"S:

THE HABIT:

YOUR "WHY"S:

THE HABIT:

YOUR "WHY"S:

THE HABIT:

YOUR "WHY"S:

THE HABIT:

YOUR "WHY"S:

THE HABIT:

YOUR "WHY"S:

THE HABIT:

YOUR "WHY"S:

THE HABIT:

YOUR "WHY"S:

THE HABIT:

YOUR "WHY"S:

THE HABIT:

YOUR "WHY"S:

THE HABIT:

YOUR "WHY"S:

THE HABIT:

YOUR "WHY"S:

THE HABIT:

YOUR "WHY"S:

THE HABIT:

YOUR "WHY"S:

THE HABIT:

YOUR "WHY"S:

THE HABIT:

YOUR "WHY"S:

THE HABIT:

YOUR "WHY"S:

THE HABIT:

YOUR "WHY"S:

THE HABIT:

YOUR "WHY"S:

THE HABIT:

YOUR "WHY"S:

THE HABIT:

YOUR "WHY"S:

THE HABIT:

YOUR "WHY"S:

THE HABIT:

YOUR "WHY"S:

THE HABIT:

YOUR "WHY"S: